FLORENCE

280 colour photographs

BONECHI EDITORE

50122 FIRENZE - Via dei Rustici, 5

THE COATS-OF-ARMS
OF THE MAJOR
AND MINOR GUILDS

Seta

Medici e Speziali

Calzolai

Correggiai

Cuoiai

Legnaioli

Fornai

Beccai

Vinattieri

Oliandoli

Albergatori

A few historical hints on the city of Florence

The origins of Florence go back to the period of the Etruscans when Fiesole an important city of Etruria built on top of a hill, dominated the valley. A group of its inhabitants went down the banks of the river to give life to a village, even if a modest one, but destined to develop because of a favorable position. This position was, however, an easy prey for enemies and invaders. As a matter of fact the Romans themselves put their tents there and founded a colony with the name of Florence, which means « destined to flourish ».

Since the first century A. D. this Roman Municipality affirms itself acquiring later a pre-eminent position among the cities of Tuscany, especially beginning from the III century A. D. as we see in the « Corrector Italiae ». It survived the most obscure periods of the Middle Ages to resurrect slowly during the period of Carolingian emperors, and becoming one of the most important centres in the peninsula, from a cultural point of view also. At first a feud of Tuscan Marquises, among whom are remembered Ugo and Matilde, Florence gained from the XI c. an ever-increasing autonomy: in 1115, at the end of fights against the clergy and the founders

of the region, the Florentine Commune is practically constituted. Ten years later the new state suppressed its rival Fiesole. Soon in the interior of the city, surrounded with new walls, appear the first contrasts between the owners of fiefs and the working classes, organized in Corporations.

The contrasts take the form of two factions: the Guelfs and the Ghibellines. The former are partisans of the pope, the latter of the Emperor. Florence has, however, a prevalence of Guelfs. It was these who from thhe end of the XIII century divided themselves into two factions: the whites and the blacks. The black party, supported by the Pontiff, in 1303 sends to exile the white party and among these Dante Alighieri is the « wandering Ghibelline ».

In the meantime Florence increased her power by fighting her rivals: Pistoia, Arezzo, Volterra, Siena. Culturally and economically also between the end of the thirteenth and the fourteenth century Florence was becoming one of Italy's most important centres. It is the age of Dante and Giotto, of the great companies of Bankers and Merchants, of the great industries of wool and silk. In the first decennia of the XIV century Florence goes through

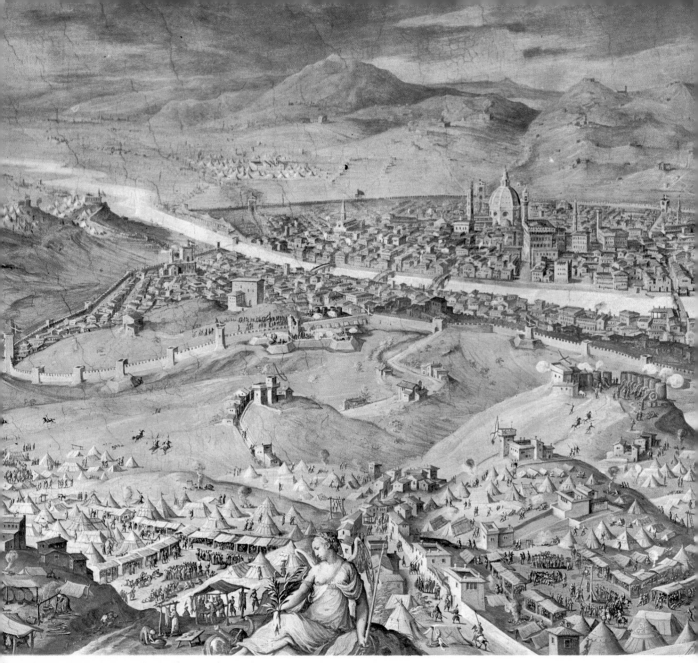

1530 Siege of Florence a fresco by Giorgio Vasari in Palazzo Vecchio

several political and economic experiences: first in the struggle against the last Ghibellines, then during the Signorie of Carlo di Calabria and Gualtieri di Brienne the Duke of Athens (1343).

The year 1348 marks the period of the plague, which is described by Boccaccio. The last decennia of the fourteenth century sees ever-growing contrasts between the « fat people », that is, the rich bourgeoisie which leads the state through the Major Arts and the « minor people ».

The fight reaches its climax in the « tumult of Ciompi » (1378), the humble workers of the Arte della Lana, through which the lower stratum of the population obtains representation. Soon enough, how-

ever, the oligarchy, led by the Albizzi, had the best of the situation. In the meantime the Medici family, leaning on the people, was gaining more and more political influence.

In a short time the Signoria was constituted, even though preserving its Republican appearances. To the founder of the Medici Signoria Cosimo the Elder, succeeded Lorenzo later called Magnificent, an acute politician and a great man. The century which culminates in the Signoria of the Magnificent is one of the most enlightened in Florentine history, especially in the cultural and artistic fields: it is the age of Humanism which has in Florence its centre. For a few more years the city remained a free

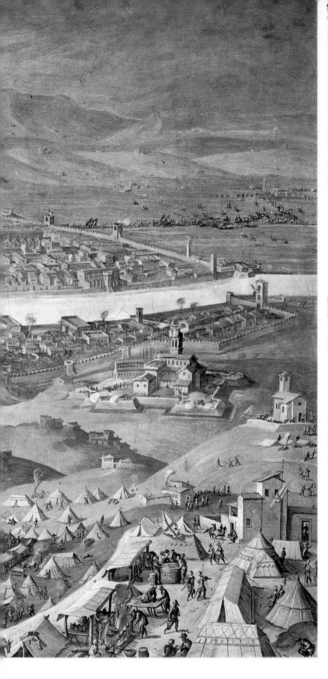

Andrea del Castagno - Farinata degli Uberti ▶

Republic: between the end of the fifteenth century and the beginning of the sixteenth century, after the expulsion of Piero the successor of Lorenzo. This glorious period is dominated by the figure of Girolamo Savonarola. Once the Medici returned, Florence was under their Signoria until 1527, when a new insurrection gave once again the much-desired Republican government to the city.

The Medicis, however, supported by the Emperor and the Pope came back after a very long siege (1530). Even during the restless political life, the years between the end of the fifteenth century and the first decennia of the sixteenth century are rich with the greatest personalities in the artistic and literary fields (Michelangelo, Machiavelli, Guicciardini). In 1569 Cosimo de' Medici, the head of the city, was given the title of Grand Duke which he passed to his successors until the extinction of the Giangastone dynasty, (1737). The successors were the Lorrain who made the Grand Duchy, except for the period of the domination of Napoleon (1799-1814), until the reunion of Florence and Tuscany with Italy (1859).

Finally Florence was the capital of Italy from 1865 to 1871.

The Old Centre

The heart of Florence's old centre is the Palazzo Vecchio, this graceful building with its battlements and slender tower, built by Arnolfo di Cambio in 1229 and inspired by the castle of the Guidi counts at Poppi. On the tower is Florence's first public clock, made in the nearly street which because of this is called Via dell'Oriuolo (« Street of the Clock »). On the left stands the bell-tower of the Badia Church, which tolled the hours in the medieval city. Next to it is the formidable mass of the Bargello: the headquarters of the chief of police, it was later used as a prison until the death penalty was abolished in Tuscany under the wise laws of Leopold I of Lorena. Condemned prisoners heard their sentences here in front of the Badia Church.

Calimala

Cambio

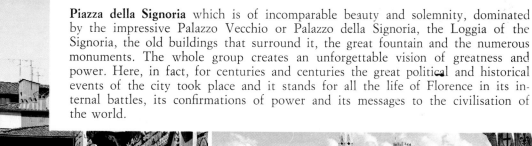

Piazza della Signoria which is of incomparable beauty and solemnity, dominated by the impressive Palazzo Vecchio or Palazzo della Signoria, the Loggia of the Signoria, the old buildings that surround it, the great fountain and the numerous monuments. The whole group creates an unforgettable vision of greatness and power. Here, in fact, for centuries and centuries the great political and historical events of the city took place and it stands for all the life of Florence in its internal battles, its confirmations of power and its messages to the civilisation of the world.

PIAZZA DELLA SIGNORIA. **Fountain of the Piazza**, by Bartolomeo Ammannati (1563-75), with its awkward gigantesque statue of Neptune, called the « Biancone » by Florentines because of its clear white mass. A work that is not excessively admired and made the Florentines say « Oh. Ammannato, Ammannato, what lovely marble you have ruined! ». The bronze statues that decorate the pool of the fountain are instead very beautiful, representing satyrs and naiads, again owed to Ammannati and others, among them Giambologna.

The Loggia of the Signoria

A rare example of late Gothic work with early Renaissance warnings.
It was also called the **Loggia of the Lanzi** because the Lanzichenecchi were stationed here in the XVI century as a guard for Cosimo I, and it was also given the name of the **Loggia dell'Orcagna,** following the supposed design by the artist. The construction was actually owed to the same architects who were in charge of the construction of the Cathedral, in other words: Benci di Cione, Simone di Francesco Talenti and others from 1376 to 1382, and was built for the elections and proclamations of the Priors and the Gonfalonier as well as other cerimonies of the Signoria. The masterpieces of sculpture underneath the loggia, belonging to various periods, make a marvellous open-air museum.

« Hercules beating the centaur Nesso » by Giambologna.

« The Rape of Polyxena » by Pio Fedi.

The statues in the Loggia della Signoria

In 1788 the antique feminine statues and the two lions on the steps at the entrance which came from the Villa Medici in Rome were placed here; beneath the first arch on the left is the « Perseus » the bronze masterpiece of Benvenuto Cellini carried out between 1545 and 1554 and immediately destined for this spot. One should note the power of the modelling and the harmony of the parts of great pictorial effect. Behind this group is the « Rape of Polyxena » a very fine nineteenth century sculpture by Pio Fedi realised in 1866; in the middle of the loggia is « Menelaus supporting the body of Patroclus », an ancient sculpture from a Greek original given to the Grand Duke Cosimo I by Pope Pius V and brought to Florence in 1579. It was placed here in 1841. Below the right-hand arch is a masterpiece by the Belgian sculptor Giambologna of the « Rape of the Sabine Women » (1583); behind this group is another lovely sculpture by the same artist « Hercules beating the centaur Nesso » carried out in 1599, and placed here in 1842.

« Menelaus supporting the body of Patroclus » from a Greek original of the IV century B.C.

« **Perseus** » by Benvenuto Cellini   « **The Rape of the Sabine Women** » by Giambologna

Over the entrance door into Palazzo Vecchio is a decorative fronton in marble with the **Monogram of Christ** between two lions and the writing « Rex Regum et Dominus dominantium » (Jesus Christ King of Kings and Lord of Lords). This inscription dates from 1551 and was requested by Cosimo I de' Medici to substitute an earlier one placed there in 1529 by the people during the famous siege and which said: « Jesus Christus, Rex Florentini Populi S. P. Decreto Electus », an inscription of clear Savonarolian impront which aroused the suspicions of the despotic Lord of Florence.

Equestrian monument of the Grand Duke Cosimo I de' Medici, the work of Giambologna in 1594, on the base are three bass reliefs with significative episodes from the life of the Grand Duke.

Important sculptures are arranged on the level space of the steps in front of the palace where orators harangued the people in olden days, because of this it was called the « Arringhiera ». From the left: **Judith and Holophernes,** a bronze by Donatello (1460) considered the symbol of liberty and placed here in memory of the expulsion of the Duke of Athens from Florence; a copy of the **David** by Michelangelo, whose original stood here from 1503 to 1873 and was then taken to the Academy Gallery; and the marble group representing **Hercules and Cacus,** by Baccio Bandinelli (1533).

Palazzo Vecchio

It represents the principal architectural monument in Florence and one of the most significant mediaeval public palaces in Italy. It rises up, majestic and severe in its power, with its tower (94 metres high) which is thrown straight up from the facade, with great clarity of construction, which gives a particular character of elegance to the whole building. According to tradition it was constructed by the genius Arnolfo di Cambio from 1298 to 1314, using the castle of the Counts Guidi di Poppi as a model, but this attribution has not been substantiated by any document. The original construction was a great parallelepiped in rough rustic work with very beautiful Gothic two lighted windows on two floors and crowned by a great parapet walk with esparto battlementing. In the front, the tower that goes by the name of Arnolfo rises up on a rectangular design, erected laterally because it was constructed on the pre-existing one of the Foraboschi, with battlemented double bow windows.

A charming view of « **Arnolfo's tower.** » In the foreground « **The Rape of the Sabine Women.** » To the right the lovely fountain in the courtyard of Palazzo Vecchio.

COURTYARD OF THE PALAZZO VEC-CHIO. — Designed by Michelozzo (1439-54). When Francesco de' Medici married Joan of Austria in 1565, Vasari decorated the courtyard with frescoes depicting scenes of Austrian cities in honour of the bride. At the same time the colums were adorned with gilt stuccoes. The porphyry basin in the centre of the courtyard is by Battista del Tadda. In 1476 Verrocchio's « Boy vith a Fish » was placed above the basin: now substituted by a copy, the original (photo at right) is in another part of the building.

HALL OF THE FIVE HUNDRED. Designed by Simone del Pollaiolo, called Il Cronaca, as the seat of the Consiglio Maggiore, Florence's governing body which was set up in 1494 on the Venetian model. Vasari painted the hall's frescoes between 1555 and 1572 while remodelling the building to make it the residence of the Medici family, who had become Grand Dukes of Florence with the accession of Cosimo I. The ceiling is divided into 39 panels. The central panel depicts the triumph of Cosimo I; others show the quarters of the city, the city itself, the various offices of the Medici, and scenes of battles for the conquest of Pisa and Siena. The long walls were to have been painted with frescoes by Michelangelo and Leonardo, though the latter did not more than the preliminary sketches. The wall at the end of the hall was constructed by Bandinelli. In the centre of it stands Michelangelo's statue of Victory, and at either side statues depicting the Labours of Hercules. Above the statues is a balcony.

The great frescoes on the walls were carried out by Vasari and depict the triumph of Cosimo I and episodes from the war of the Florentines against the Pisans and Sienese. (Above) « **The victory of Marciano** ». (Below) « **The conquest of Siena** ».

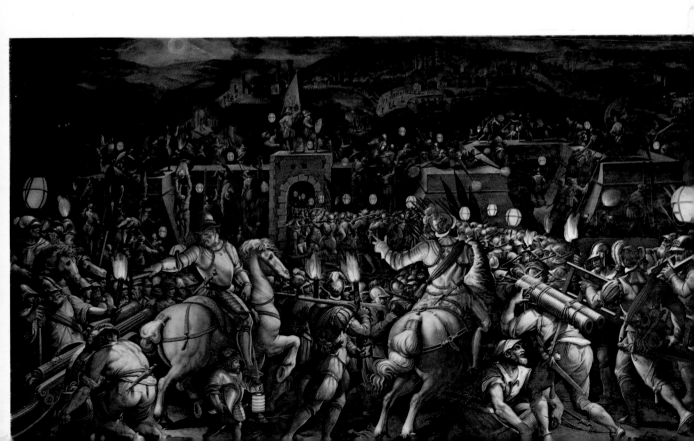

Hall of the Five Hundred. — In the top part of the photo is a representation of
the battle fought on August 17, 1505: **The florentine soldiers defeat the Pisan army at torre San Vincenzo**. Beneath, **The siege and conquest of Pisa,** a decisive
battle fought on June 8, 1509.

Studio of Francesco I. — A masterpiece by Vasari, containing bronze statues by Giambologna and portraits by Bronzino.

(Left) **« The Victory of Virtue over Brute Force »,** a marble group by Michelangelo (1525) placed in the central niche of the end wall of the Hall of the Five Hundred. Right, one of the six statues representing **« The Labours of Hercules »** along the walls, is by Vincenzo de' Rossi.

Above the **Hall of the Two Hundred**; Below the **Room of Clemente VII**, the mayor's residence; to one side the Chapel with Bronzino's frescoes.

FODERVNT MANVS MEAS ET PEDES
MEOS DINVMERAVERVNT OMNIA
OSSA MEA ◦◦◦ DAVID

MORTE MORIETVR TRIBVS DIEBVS
SOMNO SVBSCEPTO ET TVC AB
INFERIS REGRESSVS AD LVCEM VENIET
ERITHEA

The Chapel in the quarter of the Priors frescoed by Ridolfo del Ghirlandaio. To the left, the Audience Hall with its marvelous ceiling and its architectural and sculptural works by Benedetto da Maiano. The frescoes are by Salviati.

Above, the **Hall of Lilies** in the Quarters of the Priors. It takes its name from the decorations on the walls of fleur-de-lis of gold which surround the relations of the Florentine Republic with the Kingdom of France. The architecture and the lovely ceiling is by Benedetto and Giuliano da Maiano. Right, the **Medici Storeroom,** also called the **Hall of the Geographical Maps** because 33 geographical maps are painted on the cupboard doors, all owed to friar Ignazio Danti (1563-75) the great mathematician, and don Stefano Buonsignori (1575-84).

The Piazzale of the Uffizi. - Vasari was given the commission by the Grand Duke Cosimo I of the construction of the powerful building, where the Uffizi Gallery has its seat and with the idea originally of uniting government offices together there. Started in 1560, it can be considered as the finest architectural work by Vasari, and was finished off afterwards in 1580 by Alfonso Parigi and Bernardo Buontalenti.

Cimabue: Madonna Enthroned

Giotto: Madonna Enthroned

Simone Martini: Annunciation

1

2

3

4

5   6

1 - **Pisan School:** Crucifix with stories of the Passion

2 - **Giottino:** Deposition

3 - **Fra Angelico:** Coronation of the Virgin

4 - **Gentile da Fabriano:** Adoration of the Magi

5 - **Fra Angelico:** Madonna and Child

6 - **Masaccio:** Madonna and Child with St. Anne

7 - **Lorenzo Monaco:** Adoration of the Magi

7

Piero della Francesca: Portrait of Battista Sforza   **Piero della Francesca:** Portrait of Federico di Montefeltrc

Paolo Uccello: The Battle of San Romano

Filippo Lippi: Madonna and Child with Angels

Sandro Botticelli: The Birth of Venus, below Allegory of Spring, to the right, The Madonna of the Magnificat

SANDRO BOTTICELLI
LA MADONNA DEL "MAGNIFICAT"

1609

Filippo Lippi: Portrait of an Old Man

Andrea del Verrocchio: Baptism of Christ

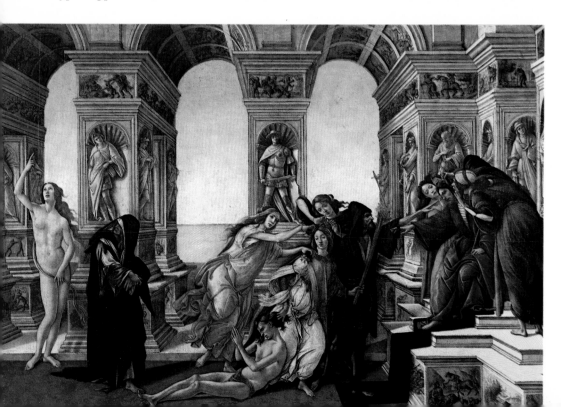

Sandro Botticelli:
Calumny

34

Domenico Ghirlandaio: Adoration of the Magi

Lukas Cranach: Adam and Eve

Rosso Fiorentino:
Musical Putto

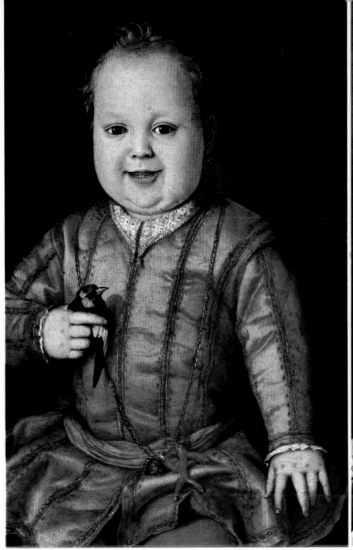

Bronzino: Portrait of Don Garzia
Leonardo da Vinci: Adoration of the Magi

Bronzino: Potrait
Andrea Mantegna: The Circumcision

THE TRIBUNE - The tribune was built by Buontalenti around 1589 to house the Medici collection. In the righthand photo, the famous « Medici Venus, » a Greek sculpture of the classical period; in the photo below, two **Greek sculptures:** « The Fighters » and « The Knife Grinder »

Leonardo da Vinci: Annunciation

Michelangelo: The Holy Family ▶

Titian: Venus of Urbino

Hugo Van der Goes: The Portinari Altarpiece

Raphael: Madonna del Cardellino   **Rosso Fiorentino:** Moses Defending the Daughters of Jethr

Bachiacca: The Story of St. Acacio

Parmigianino: Madonna of the Long Neck

Perugino: Virgin and Saints

Caravaggio: Adolescent Bacchus

The Religious Centre

The octagonal building on the right is the **Baptistery** where Florentines have been received into the Christian faith almost for as long as Florence has been Christian. It was also the first cathedral within the city walls. Then this honour fell to **Santa Reparata**, and later to the vast present-day cathedral, which is dedicated to the Madonna and called « **Santa Maria del Fiore** » (St. Mary of the Flower), thus invoking the Virgin's protection of Florence whose emblem is a flower: the lily. As recent excavantions have shown, Santa Reparata formerly stood in the site of the present Cathedral. This therefore has always been the religious centre of Florence, though its buildings have grown and changed over the centuries. From Roman times, to which the foundations of the Baptistery date back, through the Renaissance age when the cathedral was finally crowned with its huge **Cupola**, to the 19th century when the marble facade was added: this area has been the focus of the Christian faith in Florence. Beside the Cathedral: **Giotto's Bell-tower.**

The Baptistery

This is one of the oldest buildings in Florence, one which Dante remembers, calling it « my lovely San Giovanni », the place where he was baptised. Judged earlier on to be a construction of the V century, it is now held to be a Romanesque construction of the XI-XII century, built on the remains of a paleochristian monument where the remains of a Roman construction were found in the foundations. It is an example of Tuscan Romanesque architecture on an octagonal plan with coloured marbles, and surrounded by a double order of pilasters which support the arches. The covering of the dome is hidden by an attic (XIII century). It was consacrated to St. John the Baptist and was cathedral of Florence until 1128. The three entrance doors which are of exceptional interest, are placed according to the cardinal points.

In the interior of the Baptistery, the chancel arch of the apse and the dome are a splendour of Byzantine style mosaics of the XIII-XIX century, carried out by Venetian and Florentine artists. The mosaics of the tribune were started in 1225 by the master Iacopo da Torrita. Those of the dome are of the XIV century, to which Cimabue, Andrea di Riccio called Tafo and Gaddo Gaddi contributed.

Lorenzo Ghiberti's « Door of Paradise » took 27 years to complete (1425-1452). Old and New Testament scenes are represented in the panels.

Creation of Adam and Eve; The Original Sin; Expulsion from Paradise.

Adam and Eve with Cain and Abel; The Sacrifice to God; the first work: Abel shepherd, Cain at the plough; Cain kills Abel; First example of justice: the Curse of Cain.

Story of Noah: His family leaves the ark after the Flood; Noah's thanksgiving and the Rainbow; The planting of the Vine and Noah's drunkenness; derided by Ham he is covered by Shem.

Story of Abraham; Sara at the entrance to the tent; Angels appear to Abraham in the valley of Mambre; journey with Isaac to the Mountain; Angel holds Abraham's arm; The servants await.

Story of Jacob and Esau: Esau sells his first birthright; Isaac sends Esau hunting; Jacob brings the meat to his Father and covers his neck with the skin; Isaac mistakes Jacob for Esau and blesses him; Jacob leaves his Father's house.

Story of Joseph: He is put by his brothers in the well; Is sold to the merchants; Is sold by the merchants to Pharaon; Whose dreams he interprets and foretells the coming famine, counsels provisions; He recognises his brothers and pardons them; Meeting of Joseph and Jacob.

Story of Moses: He receives the Tablets of the Law; Joshua waits half way up the mountain; The Israelites wait in fear and trembling at the foot.

Story of Joshua: The crossing of the Jordan; The twelve stone taken from the river; The fall of the walls of Jerico; The Israelites take the city.

Story of Saul and David: Saul conquers the Phili-stines; David kills Goliath and exulting carries the head to the Army.

King Salomon solemnly receives the Queen of Sheba.

Lorenzo Ghiberti

Vittorio Ghiberti

The Cathedral (S. Maria del Fiore)

The grandiose building was started by Arnolfo di Cambio in 1296, having the commission from the Republic to carry out the work « with the most high and sumptuous magnificence so that it is impossible to make it either better or more beautiful with the industry and power of man », in the place where the church of Santa Reparata, the cathedral of Florence had been, and facing San Giovanni. On the death of Arnolfo, which came about in 1302, the works were interrupted and taken over in 1357 under the direction of Giotto, who was already supervising the realisation of the belltower. He died in 1337, and the work suffered a slowing down and from 1357 to 1364 the Cathedral Works Committee entrusted the direction to Lapo Ghini and Francesco Talenti, committing them with a project which was more grandiose than that of Arnolfo. Finally, in 1366 a definite plan was submitted by four architects and the construction continued with an easier rythm. In 1378 the vault of the middle nave were already completed, and from 1380 to 1421 the empore and the tambour of the dome were constructed. In 1436 Pope Eugenius IV solemnly consecrated the temple, dedicating to Santa Maria del Fiore. The facade was erected by the Florentine architect Emilio de Fabris who was inspired by Florentine Gothic style, continuing the construction from 1871 to 1883 and decorating it with statues carried out by contemporary artists.

The Cathedral's facing in marble of three colors: white marble from Carrara, green from Prato, and red from the Maremma region. On the **façade** inside the niches are 12 statues of the Apostles, with the Virgin and Child in the center. On either side of the portals are four statues representing the bishops who blessed the first stone, the first pier, and the façade; the third to the left is Pope Eugene IV who consecrated the church.

The Interior of the Cathedral. - Magnificent example of Gothic-Florentine architecture is vast and sober of decoration and it suits the character of the Florentines themselves who want the house of God without gracefulness, but grandiose and austere and where the people can enter in great numbers. The cathedral vault has recently undergone difficult and important excavations. The work has brought to light the structures and all that was left of the antique cathedral of Santa Reparata, which was demolished in 1296. In the photo on the left: a view of part of the crypt. Above, a fresco representing « The Resurrection », by the school of Giotto; below, a tomb stone discovered during the excavations.

CATHEDRAL - **Domenico di Michelino:** Dante and His Poem

Michelangelo: The Pietà. Now in the Cathedral, this work was sculpted by Michelangelo for his own tomb

54

The Dome. - During the construction of the Cathedral in 1418, a competition was announced for the building of the dome, won by Filippo Brunelleschi who carried out the marvellous architectural masterpiece from 1420 to 1434, and it is the admiration of the world today. Michelangelo himself was inspired by this masterpiece to construct the dome of St. Peter's in Rome. It is 91 metres high without the lantern, 114 with the lantern and 45,52 metres in diameter above the tambour. From the terrace of the parapet walk, 107 metres above ground, one can enjoy a vast and very beautiful panorama.

Giotto's Belltower. - 81,75 metres high even today it remains of a beauty that has no competitors in all the world, after more than half a millennium since its construction. In 1334, at the invitation of the Signoria, Giotto presented his designs and the foundations of the colossal work, and the building was started in July of the same year. Unfortunately, it was three years to the day after this that Giotto died and the work was continued until 1384 by Andrea Pisano and finished off by Francesco Talenti in 1359. However, both of them scrupulously followed the designs of the great master, except for the terminal spire which was never constructed and would have added another thirdy metres or so to height of the belltower. A very lovely panorama of the city and the hills that surround it can be enjoyed from the terrace at which one arrives after having climbed 414 steps.

PIAZZA SAN LORENZO —
At the centre of the popular
market (which dates from
1870 when Florence was the
capital of Italy) is the statue
of Giovanni delle Bande Ne-
re, done by Baccio Bandinelli
in 1540. The church was originally dedicated to San Lorenzo in 393 by St. Ambrose,
bishop of Milan, and for this
reason it is also known as the
Ambrosian Basilica. It assumed its present form in 1423
when rebuilt by Brunelleschi,
commissioned by Giovanni di
Bicci de' Medici. Later Michelangelo built the Chapels containing the Medici tombs and
the library, and finished the
inside of the church's facade.
He designed the outside of
the facade but this work was
never carried out.

Aerial view of the Medici - San Lorenzo complex. So called because in the 15th century it became the property of the Medici family. Clearly visible are the internal cloister, the library to one side, the domes, and the bell-tower, a later addition built by order of the last descendant of the Medici, the Palatine Elector, Maria Ludovica. On the right is the central building of the Markets. On the left is the Church of Santa Maria Novella and the central railway station. The trees in the distance belong to the Park of the Cascine with the rececourse in the centre.

Linaioli e Rigattieri

Vaiai e Pellicciai

Spadai e Corrazzai

Chiavaioli

Medici Chapel

Right, Piazza Madonna degli Aldobrandini, where the entrance of the Medici Chapels is situated. Below, the **New Sacristy,** by Michelangelo (1520-33) in the Medici Chapels. - The great Michelangelo wanted to give a grandiose and solemn feeling in the architectural parts as much as the sculptural parts. Here the three famous tombs, of which only two have been completely finished, can be found. Michelangelo sculpted only the Madonna and Child for the unfinished one. This magnificent masterpiece shows us Michelangelo as an architect as well as a sculptor. One could say that they both amount to the same thing as one cannot admire each individual work on its own, but must look at them as an inseparable whole, where architecture and sculpture are based and completed by one another. The quadrangular room with the powerful dome is full of movement and every architectural element shows up the plastic energy of the mass.

The Tomb of Giuliano Duke of Nemours, by Michelangelo. Giuliano is represented seated and wearing the armour and staff of command, a symbol of action; at his feet are the two symbolic figures that represent Day and Night.

The Night.   The Day.

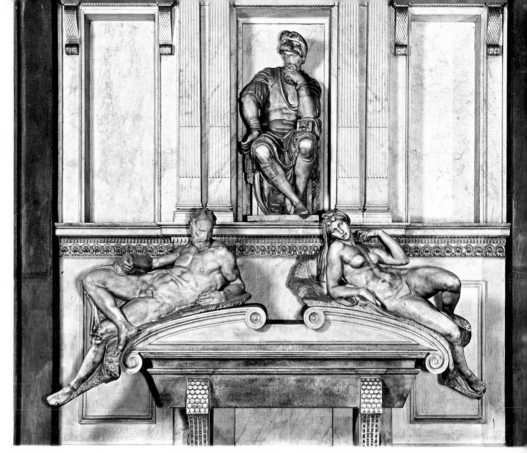

The Tomb of Lorenzo Duke of Urbino, by Michelangelo. The Duke of Urbino, grandson of Lorenzo the Magnificent, is represented in a thoughtful pose with two figures on the sarcophagus symbolising Dawn und Dusk.

The Dusk.

The Dawn.

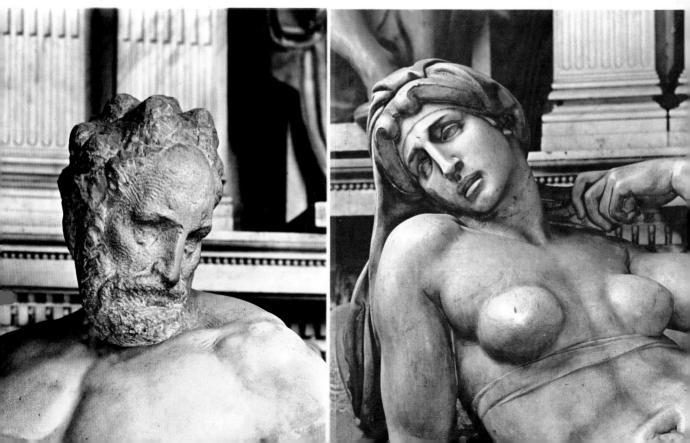

Details from Michelangelo's works. Left:: **The statue of Julius, Duke of Nemours.** Right: **The statue of Lorenzo, Duke of Urbino.** Below: **The Virgin and Child.**

The Chapel of the Princes in the Medici Chapels. - The construction of this wonderful building was started in 1604 by Matteo Nigetti from a design by Prince Giovanni de' Medici, who wished to have the sepulchre of the Medici family constructed here and worthy of their power and riches. In fact is was called the chapel of the Princes. The walls are completely covered in precious marbles, finely prepared « pietra dura » (hard stone) and gilded bronzes. The six porphyry sarcophagi belong to the Medici grand dukes from Cosimo I to Cosimo III. The bronze statues are by Pietro Tacca (XVII century).

Piazza Santa Maria Novella. — The church, designed by the friars Sisto and Ristoro, with its facade added by Leon Battista Alberti, stands at the end of this oval-shaped square with a garden in the middle. A famous carriage race was held around the square in the era of Florence's Grand Dukes. In fact the Medici Grand Duke, Cosimo I, had the obelisks placed at each end of the square to mark the limits of the course.

The Cloisters of S. Maria Novella. - The great Spanish c h a p e l: detail of « The Church Militant », by Andrea di Bonaiuto known as Andrea da Firenze (1366-68).

SANTA MARIA NOVELLA. — A church of the Dominican order, once dedicated to the education of the young (both Cimabue and Dante studied here). It stands on the former site of a smaller church called Santa Maria tra le Vigne, whence the name of Santa Maria Novella (that is « New Saint Mary's »). Begun in 1279 by two friars of the order, its overall structure was completed in 1348 by a third friar, Jacopo Talenti. It is in the Tuscan Gothic style, an shows how the soaring vertical lines which were such a central feature of Gothic architecture in northern Europe were modified in Italy by the solid, square lines of the Romanesque style, especially in Tuscany. But **the facade**, both in its form and in the delicate patterns of the marble, belongs to the Renaissance era and the unmistakable genius of Leon Battista Alberti: along with the Palazzo Rucellai, it is without doubt the masterpiece of this architect and man of letters. The church's plan is in the form of a Greek cross: inside there are chapels along the sides of the naves and transept, and slim pillars supporting Gothic pointed arches.

THE CHURCH OF CESTELLO. The lovely brick dome was put up by Antonio Ferri in 1668.

THE CHURCH OF SS. ANNUNZIATA. One of the first Renaissance works, the church was designed by the great Filippo Brunelleschi who began building it in 1421. In the middle of the square is the Equestrian Statue of Grand-duke Ferdinand I by Giambologna.

THE CHURCH OF SANTO SPIRITO. Another Renaissance work by Filippo Brunelleschi, who began it in 1444.

THE CHURCH OF OGNISSANTI (ALL SAINTS).

The church, whose origins go back to the 13th century, was rebuilt in the 17th century with a Baroque style façade. Sandro Botticelli is buried inside.

FOUNDLING HOSPITAL. Stupendous architectural work designed by Filippo Brunelleschi. In the medallions between the arches are ten glazed terracottas of swaddled babes by Andrea Della Robbia.

THE CHURCH OF SAN MARCO.

Built at the end of the 13th century, it underwent several transformation up to 1678 when, with the final changes, it assumed its present form.

PIAZZA S. TRINITA, with the Column of Justice in the centre and surrounded by ancient palaces.

PONTE S. TRINITA. - This is the most impressive bridge over the Arno. Constructed by Bartolomeo Ammannati in 1567-69 under the influence of Michelangelo, the result was one of the loveliest bridge of italian architecture. Destroyed by bombing during the war on the night of August 4th 1944, it was faithfully reconstructed « as it was and where it was », using much of the materials saved.

BRIDGES OVER THE ARNO. — In the foreground is the **Bridge of Santa Trinita** by Bartolomeo Ammannati — though it was inspired (some even say designed) by Michelangelo. Behind it the **Ponte Vecchio** (« Old Bridge ») with the little shops, now occupied by goldsmiths, clinging to its sides. At left the Palazzo Vecchio tower.

PALAZZO STROZZI. — Now used for important cultural events and exhibitions, such as that of the antique dealers, the building was begun in 1489 by Benedetto da Maiano, on a commission from the wealthy banker Filippo Strozzi. The courtyard and cornice were completed by Il Cronaca. The splendid wrought-iron lanterns at the sides are by Caparra.

THE WILD BOAR. — A bronze fountain copied by Tacca from a Hellenistic original in the Uffizi Gallery in 1612. Since then Tacca's work itself has also been transferred to the gallery. The Florentines misleadingly call the statue « the little pig ». It refers to a popular fable about a young prince who is changed into a boar by a spell and falls in love with a frog.

The Davanzati Palace

The Palace of the Wool Guild

The Church of Orsanmichele

Maestri di pietra e di legname

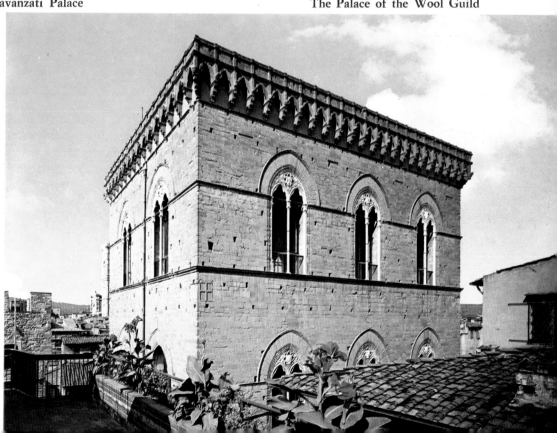

Detail of the *Court of the Magi Kings*, by Benozzo Gozzoli in the chapel of the Medici-Riccardi Palace.

THE MEDICI-RICCARDI PALACE. - This superb building of pure Renaissance character, was commissioned by Cosimo the Elder to Michelozzo Michelozzi (1444-60) student of Brunelleschi, who made his architectural masterpiece here. Later it was Lorenzo the Magnificent's royal palace.

Another splendid view of the bridges over the Arno. In the foreground the **Ponte alla Carraia** (« Wagon Bridge »), so called because it was once used by wagons entering and leaving the city. Beyond it the **Bridge of Santa Trinita** and the **Ponte Vecchio**, with its three arches. In the background on the hill, the imposing mass of the Forte di Belvedere.

The statues of **Sprin** and **Summer** at the beginning of the Santa Trinita Br

76

The Ponte Vecchio

It is so called because it is the oldest bridge in Florence and was already in existance in the time of the Etruscans. The construction in wood, built in 972, was destroyed by the river in flood in 1333. It was then reconstructed in stone in 1345 by Neri di Fioravante who gave it its present characteristics with the shops along the sides. Originally these

the XVI century, at the wish of Cosimo I, they were assigned to gold and silversmith: even today the tradition is respected a good deal. High up, on the left side, runs the famous Vasari corridor which links the Uffizi Gallery with the Pitti Palace.

shops were rented to butchers; but in

THE PONTE VECCHIO. — A view of its typical little shops from the far side of the Arno. The bridge is called « Vecchio » (« old ») because it is the most ancient of all the bridges over the Arno.

PITTI PALACE. - It is the most monumental of all the palaces in Florence. The building, on a design by Filippo Brunelleschi, was constructed in the middle of the XV century and was ordered by Luca Pitti, a very rich merchant and antagonist of the Medici family, who wanted a palace that in size would be bigger than all the other existing ones, and not only that, but it had to have its windows as big as the portal of the Medici palace in Via Larga (that is the Medici-Riccardi Palace in Via Cavour). Brunelleschi designed the central part keeping to the Renaissance spirit of measured equilibrium, in simple but grandiose forms, in three graded floors in rustic style and opened out by arches. In 1465, when the Pitti family fell into ruin, the costruction was interrupted. In 1549 the palace was bought by Eleonora di Toledo the wife of Cosimo I, who gave the commission to Bartolomeo Ammannati of carrying out the work of completing

Fra Bartolomeo:
Deposition

Filippo Lippi:
Madonna and Child

Antonio Van Dyke: Cardinal Bentivoglio

Murillo: Madonna and Child

Sodoma: St. Sebastian

Raphael: Lady with a Veil

Andrea del Sarto:
Stories from the life
of St. Joseph

82

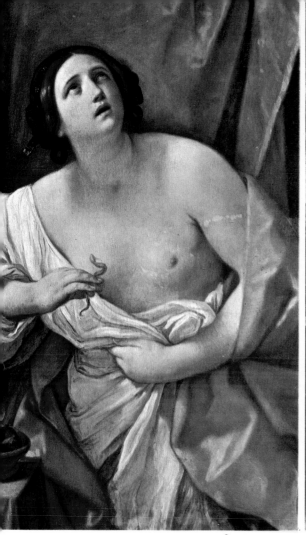

Guido Reni: Cleopatra   **Velasquez:** Portrait of Philip IV of Spain

Raphael: Agnolo and
Maddalena Doni

Godfried Schalken: Girl with a Light

Domenico Feti: The Lost Drachma

Pontormo: Adoration of the Magi

Raph
The Madonna of the C

RAFFAELLO SANZIO

N. AD URBINO 6 APRILE 1483
M. A ROMA 6 APRILE 1520

MADONNA DELLA SEGGIOLA

Andrea del Sarto: St. Sebastian

Sustermans: Prince Mattias de' Medici

Titian: Concert

Raphael: Cardinal Bernardo Dovizi   **Sustermans:** Waldemaro Cristiano di Danimarca

Francesco Botticini:
Madonna and Child with Angels

Empoli: Still Life

Raphael: Madonna of the Grand-duke

Titian: Philip II of Spain

Volterrano: Pievano Arlotto's Joke

Titian: The Englishman

Pietro Paolo Rubens: The Four Philosophers

Perugino: Madonna of the Sack

Pitti Palace. - **Throne Room.**

The **Dining-room** in ▶
the ex-royal appart-
ments of the Pitti Pa-
lace.

Panoramic view of the
Boboli **Amphitheater.**
In the foreground one
of the wings of the
Pitti Palace.

Boboli Gardens. — The Isolotto pond. On the island in the middle is the Fountain of the Ocean, by Alfonso Parigi, which includes a copy with variations of Giambologna's statue of Neptune in Bologna. Emerging from the water are Adromeda and Perseus. Around the fountain are statues representing the Nile, Ganges and Euphrates rivers.

The Fountain of Bacchino: renowned for the curious little figure which is said to be a portrait of Cosimo I's famous dwarf.

Panoramic view of the **Boboli Gardens.**

Florence

by night

From the ramps leading up to Piazzale Michelangelo. In the foreground the San Niccolo Gate. The photo below shows the city seen from the opposite side.

PIAZZA SANTA CROCE. - It is the square which has followed the evolution of the real city: from the first meetings of the people who listened to the voices of the preachers of the faith of Christ, to the fifteenth-century knights' joust, among which was that won by Giuliano de' Medici and immortalised by the verses of Poliziano, and the sixteenth century disputes over the football games in which the Florentine people took part, at any rate in spirit.

The church of **S. Croce** is one of the most fa-mous Franciscan churches in Italy. The construction was started in the second half of the XIII century and finished at the end of the XIV century. It is a masterpiece of Florentine Gothic architecture, attributed to the genius of Anolfo di Cambio, the same architect as that of Palazzo della Signoria and the cathedral. The marble facade is the modern work of Niccolò Matas (1857-63). The fine bell-tower, which repeats Gothic style, is the work of Gaetano Baccani (1847).

Santa Croce

Tomb of Michelangelo.
— Created by Vasari in 1564, its statues symbolise Painting, Sculpture and Architecture.

S. Croce. - The interior is on an Egyptian cross divided into three naves by elegant pilasters and pointed arches. The ceiling, as in all Franciscan churches, has a roof covering of uncovered roof trusses. The walls were once completely decorated with frescoes by Giotto and his helpers which could have reached up until our times, if Giorgio Vasari at the order of Cosimo I in the XVI century, had not had them plastered over and altars of little value placed on the walls in the concept of rearranging the church. From earliest times the Florentines had themselves buried in this church, attracted by the new and profound word of the order that preached poverty, humility and castity, against the opposing customs of the time: little by little the church became a great cemetery in this way. Members of noble Florentine families and personalities from the life of the times, came here in great numbers to seek their eternal repose.

The Chair by Benedetto da Maiano (1476).

« **Annunciation** » by Donatello (1435).

« **Exequies of St. Francis** » by Giotto (1317).

Taddeo Gaddi's **Crucifix** which is in the Sacristy

Cimabue's famous **Crucifix** before the November 4, 1966 flood which irreparably damaged it as the photo below shows.

PIAZZA SAN FIRENZE. - A suggestive square which is typically Florentine. The beautiful view of the Bargello Palace which rises severely up like a fortilice, with its thirteenth century tower against which is the fine and acute belfry of the Badia Fiorentina. In the background, the cathedral with Brunelleschi's dome. On the right-hand page, above, the **Palazzo del Bargello.** It is so called because towards the end of the sixteenth century the Captain of Justice called Bargello, established himself there; together with the justices of Rota. The construction, started in 1256 and namely 43 years before the Palazzo della Signoria, was in the beginning used as the seat of the Captain of the People, then of the mayor. The palace now holds the National Museum. In the lower photo is the very beautiful **Courtyard**, irregular because of the arrangement of the various architectural elements, rich with suggestive charm for its harmony which results and for the crowding of the images which are roused by its history.

1   2   3

NATIONAL MUSEUM. Situated in the Palazzo del Bargello, which was once the city prison. The ground floor has now been converted into an « armoury » with glass cases containing arquebuses, pistols, sabres and suits of armour. On the upper floors is a rich collection of sculpture; pictured here are: I, **The Young David** (Donatello); 2, **St. George** (Donatello), formerly in the tabernacle of the Church of Orsanmichele; 3, **The Young David** (Verrocchio); 4, **San Giovannino** (Donatello), formerly in the Casa Martelli; 5, **Athys** (Donatello); 6, **Bacchus** (Michelangelo). In the **Maiolica Room** is a collection of terracotta works, formerly in the Medici residence, by the Della Robbia brothers, Luca, Andrea and Giovanni. They include the tondo (at right) of the **Madonna and Child Among Saints,** framed by the characteristc festoon of flowers. The glazing process used in their ceramic work by this famous family of artists — of whom the greatest is Luca — remains a secret to this day.

5

6

National Museum

Donatello: David

Michelangelo: Bust of Brutus

Michelangelo: Madonna and Child

Benvenuto Cellini: Cosimo I de' Medici

Andrea Della Robbia: Madonna of the Architects

Luca Della Robbia:
Madonna and Child
with Angels

Two charming aerial views of the city.

Panoramic view of Florence with the Cathedral and Palazzo Vecchio standing out.

St. Mark Museum

The museum is situated in the ancient building which was originally the convent of the Vallombrosian friars and later of the Silvestrines. By order of Cosimo the Elder, the convent was completely rebuilt by Michelozzo between 1437 and 1457. At this time it had already been allotted to the Dominicans from Fiesole, one of whom was Giovanni, called Beato Angelico, who lived there from 1435 until 1445. The museum has a large collection of paintings by Beato Angelico, and all his works contain the purpose of the glorification of faith, of perpetual adoration and of the mystical exhaltation of the Divine Love. The figure above represents the great, drammatic and yet seraphic composition of the « Crucifixion »; on the right-hand page: « The Descent from the Cross ».

POSTQUAB CONSVMATI SVNT DIES OCTO VT CIRCVCIDERET PVER VOCATV E NOM ES IHES. LVCE. II. C.

ELONGAVI FVGIENS 7 MANSI INSOLITVDINE. PS. XXXXXV. C

SVRGE ACCIPE PVERVM 7 MATREM. ET 7 FVGE INEGIPTVM. MACEI. II. C.

Fra Angelico: Flight into Egypt

The luminous « **Tribune** » built by the architect Emilio de Fabris, to house the famous statue of « **Davd** » which once stood in front of the Palazzo Vecchio but was brought here for preservation purposes in 1873. Below: « **The Adimari-Ricasoli wedding-feast in Piazza S. Giovanni** » (the Duomo Square) on the front of a fifteenth-century coffer showing a lively scene with Florentine costumes of that period.

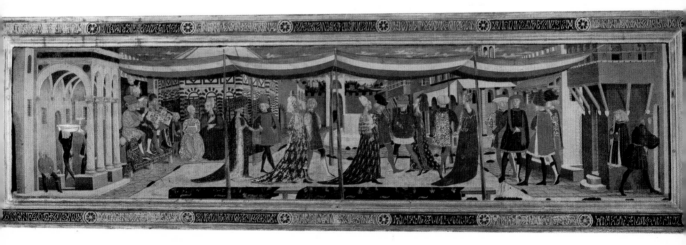

The « **David** » by Michelangelo. The Florentine Republic entrusted Michelangelo with the creation of a symbol of freedom which was to be placed in front of the Palazzo Vecchio, but which has now been replaced by a copy. It is a work done in the youth of the artist who was 26 years old when he started to sculpt it and he finished it in four years (1501-4). This gigantic youthful figure is very beautiful and its pride and virility, physical loveliness and nobility of expression tell us how much Michelangelo adhered to the symbol conceived.

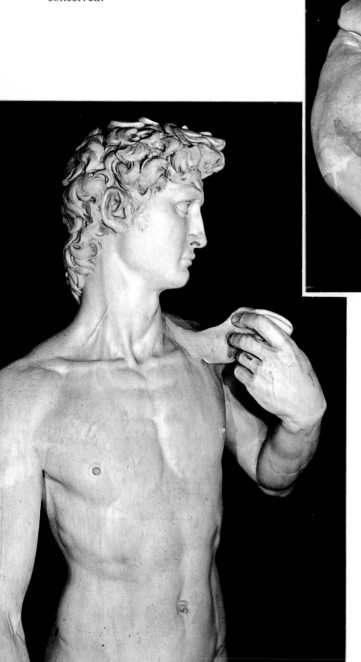

Two « **Prisoners** » by Michelangelo. This gallery houses the very famous « prisoners », four roughly-hewn sculptures which, together with the others housed in the Louvre museum in Paris, were meant for the tomb of Julius II in Rome (1518) which the artist planned but never finished. On the right-hand page: « **The Palestrina Pietà** » by Michelangelo who sculpted it late in life for the Barberini Chapel at Palestrina.

The Sinagogue, erected in 1872-74. In oriental style it has a lovely dome covered in copper and the windows are remarkably designed.

Left: the church of S. Maria del Carmine where we find the Brancacci Chapel with the famous series of frescoes begun by Masolino (1424-25) continued by Masaccio (1426-27) and finally completed by Filippino Lippi (1481-85). On the right-hand page, above: the inside of the Brancacci Chapel and the fresco representing the « Expulsion of Adam and Eve from Paradise » by Masaccio. Below: « The Payment of the Tribute » by Masaccio.

The Piazzale Michelangelo

It constitutes the most suggestive point of the celebrated trip around the Viale dei Colli. From the great terrace the eye can take in most of the panorama of the city, cut in two by the Arno, and the hills that surround it. In the centre of the square stands a monument dedicated to Michelangelo with a synthesis of the most famous sculptural works by the incomparable master; the David stands in the centre and the four statues that adorn the Medici sepulchre in the Chapel of San Lorenzo are around the pedestal (1875). This marvellous addition to the beauties of Florence is the work of the architect Giuseppe Poggi who idealised and costructed it in 1868. At the opposite end the square, on a wall preceded by a little garden has been placed a great epitaph: « Giuseppe Poggi - Florentine architect - look around - here is his monument ».

THE CHURCH OF ST. MINIATO AL MONTE. - It rises out of the hill at Monte alle Croci, preceded by a vast square from which there is a magnificent view of Florence and the surrounding hills. The church is of Florentine-Romanesque architecture, begun in the 11th century and finished in the 13th century, quite typical with its facade of white and dark green marble. The lower half has fine large arches, while the upper part is divided into three by columns, with a central spandrel window surmounted by a mosaic (see photo, left). Interior, with three naves divided by columns (see photo above). Of particular interest are: the Tabernacle of the Crucifixion by Michelozzo (1448); the Sacristy, entirely frescoed by Spinello Aretino towards the end of the 14th century; the mosaic in the apse vault and the Cardinal of Portugal's Chapel, erected by Antonio Manetti between 1461 and 1466 for the Cardinal Archbishop of Lisbon, Jacob of Lusitania, which houses works by Antonio Rossellino, Luca della Robbia and Alessio Baldovinetti.

FORT BELVEDERE or **Fort San Giorgio.** - It was constructed in 1590-95 by Bernardo Buontalenti from a design by Giovanni de' Medici and at the wish of the Grand Duke Ferdinando I. The construction is formed by a central building and grandiose glacis from which one can enjoy a magnificent panoramic view over the city and the surrounding hills. In order to arrive at Palazzina di Belvedere, where the rooms have been adapted for exhibitions of art and manifestations of a touristic character, one has to climb up a steep corridor, where cannons were dragged once upon a time, and which opens out onto a terrace.

Via San Leonardo

Fiesole. - The characteristic Via S. Francesco that leaves from Piazza Mino da Fiesole and leads, climbing steeply, up to the square of the hill of S. Francesco.

View of the **Piazza Mino da Fiesole** with the equestrian monument representing G. Garibaldi and Victor Emmanuel II, the king of Italy.

The facade of the church of San Francesco with its over-
hanging porch surmounted by a rose window.

The Roman Theatre, dating from the beginning of the
Imperial period. In the background is the characteristic
battlemented belltower of the cathedral.

INDEX

*Finito di stampare nel Giugno 1975
dalle Arti Grafiche Parigi & Maggiorelli, Firenze*